I0817230

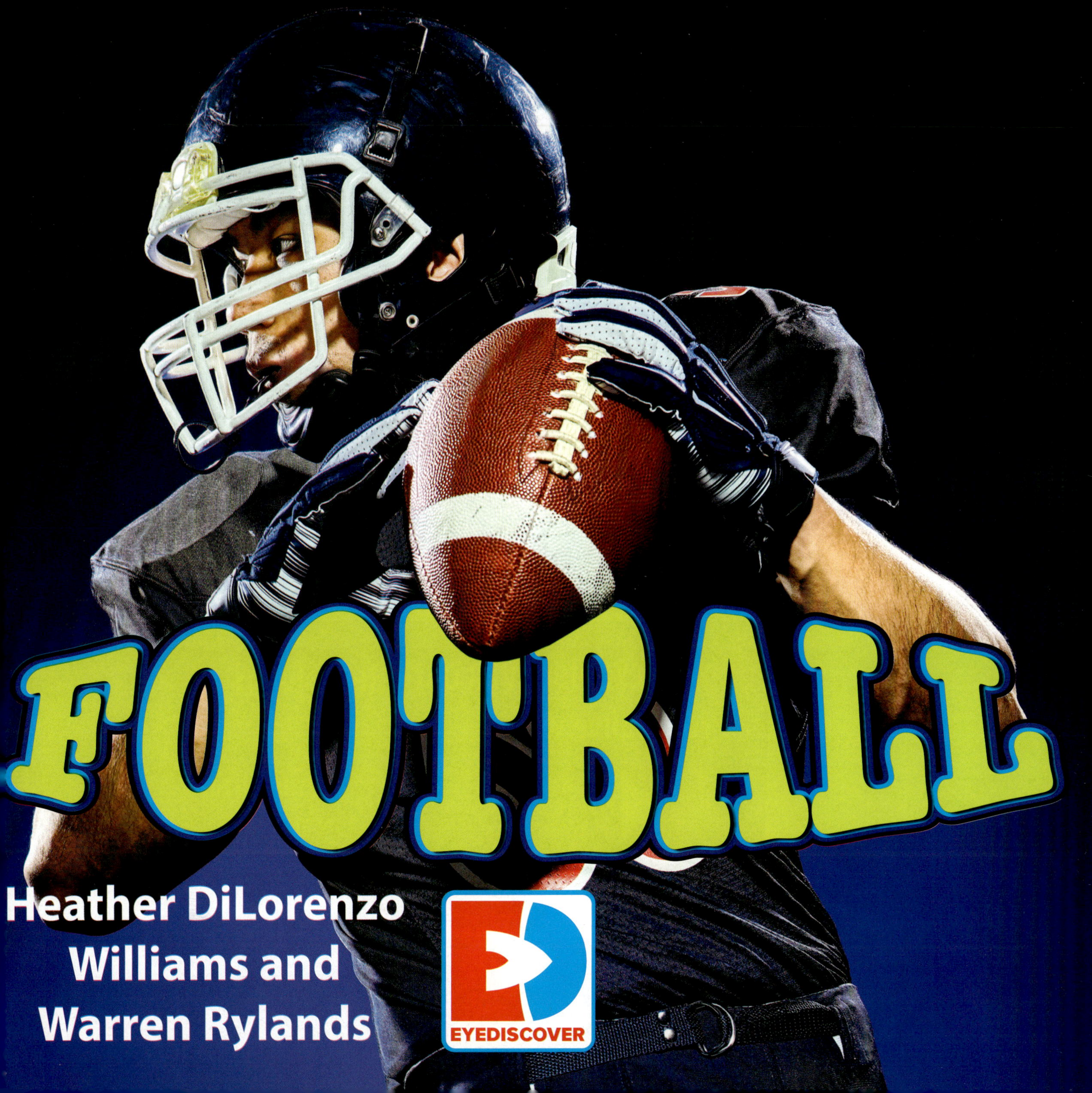
FOOTBALL
Heather DiLorenzo
Williams and
Warren Rylands
EYEDISCOVER

Go to www.eyediscover.com and enter this book's unique code.

BOOK CODE

AVM75328

EYEDISCOVER brings you optic readalongs that support active learning.

Published by AV² by Weigl
350 5th Avenue, 59th Floor New York, NY 10118
Website: www.eyediscover.com

Library of Congress Control Number: 2018953519

ISBN 978-1-4896-8031-0 (hardcover)

Printed in Brainerd, Minnesota,United States
1 2 3 4 5 6 7 8 9 0 22 21 20 19 18

082018
120917

Project Coordinators: John Willis
Designer: Mandy Christiansen

Weigl acknowledges Alamy, Getty Images, and iStock as the primary image suppliers for this title.

EYEDISCOVER provides enriched content, optimized for tablet use, that supplements and complements this book. EYEDISCOVER books strive to create inspired learning and engage young minds in a total learning experience.

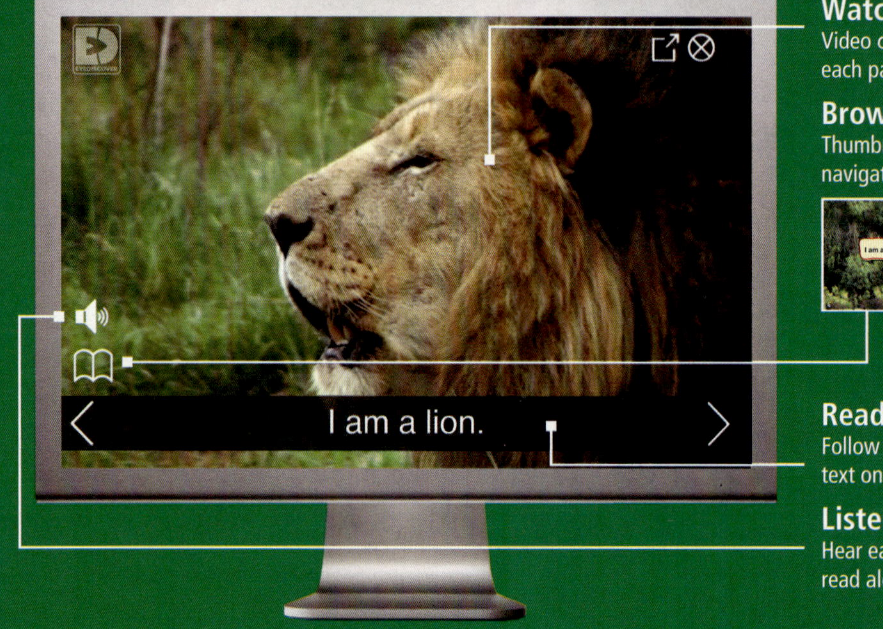

Watch
Video content brings each page to life.

Browse
Thumbnails make navigation simple.

Read
Follow along with text on the screen.

Listen
Hear each page read aloud.

Your EYEDISCOVER Optic Readalongs come alive with...

Audio
Listen to the entire book read aloud.

Video
High resolution videos turn each spread into an optic readalong.

OPTIMIZED FOR

- TABLETS
- WHITEBOARDS
- COMPUTERS
- AND MUCH MORE!

FOOTBALL

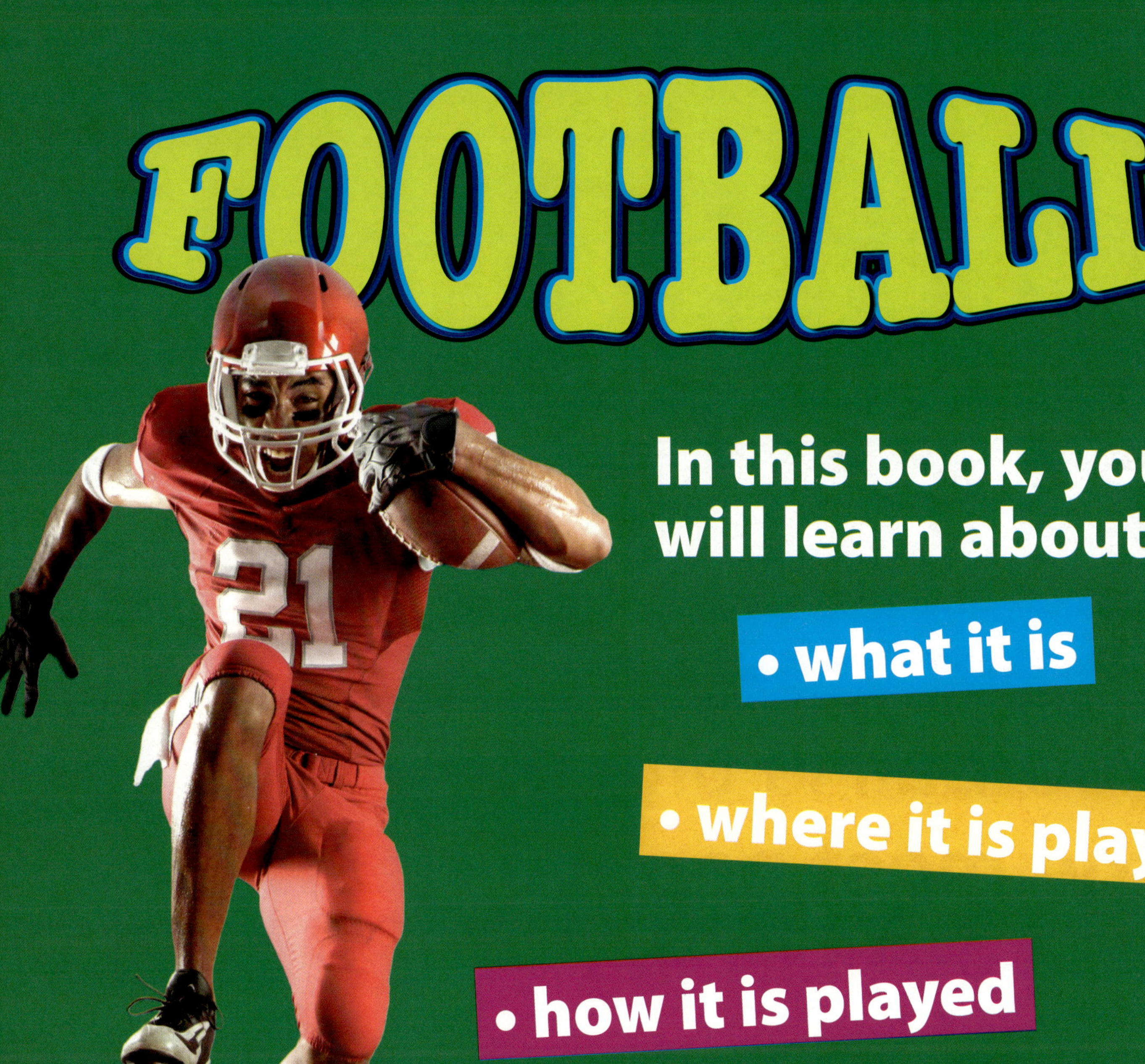

In this book, you will learn about

- what it is
- where it is played
- how it is played

and much more!

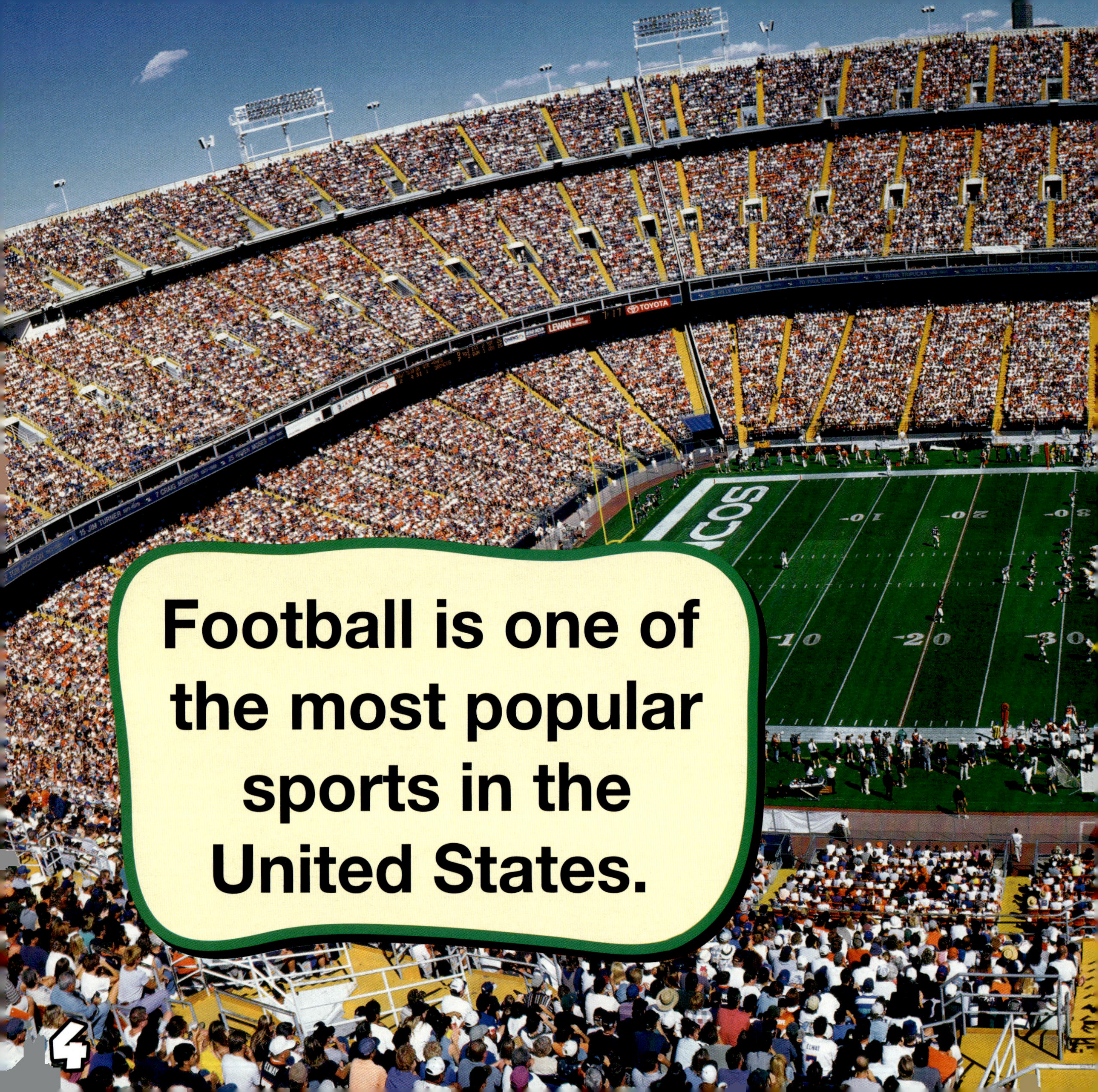

Football is one of the most popular sports in the United States.

BRONCOS

Football is a contact sport. Players wear pads and a helmet to protect their bodies and heads.

Football is played by kicking, throwing, catching, and carrying the ball.

22

81

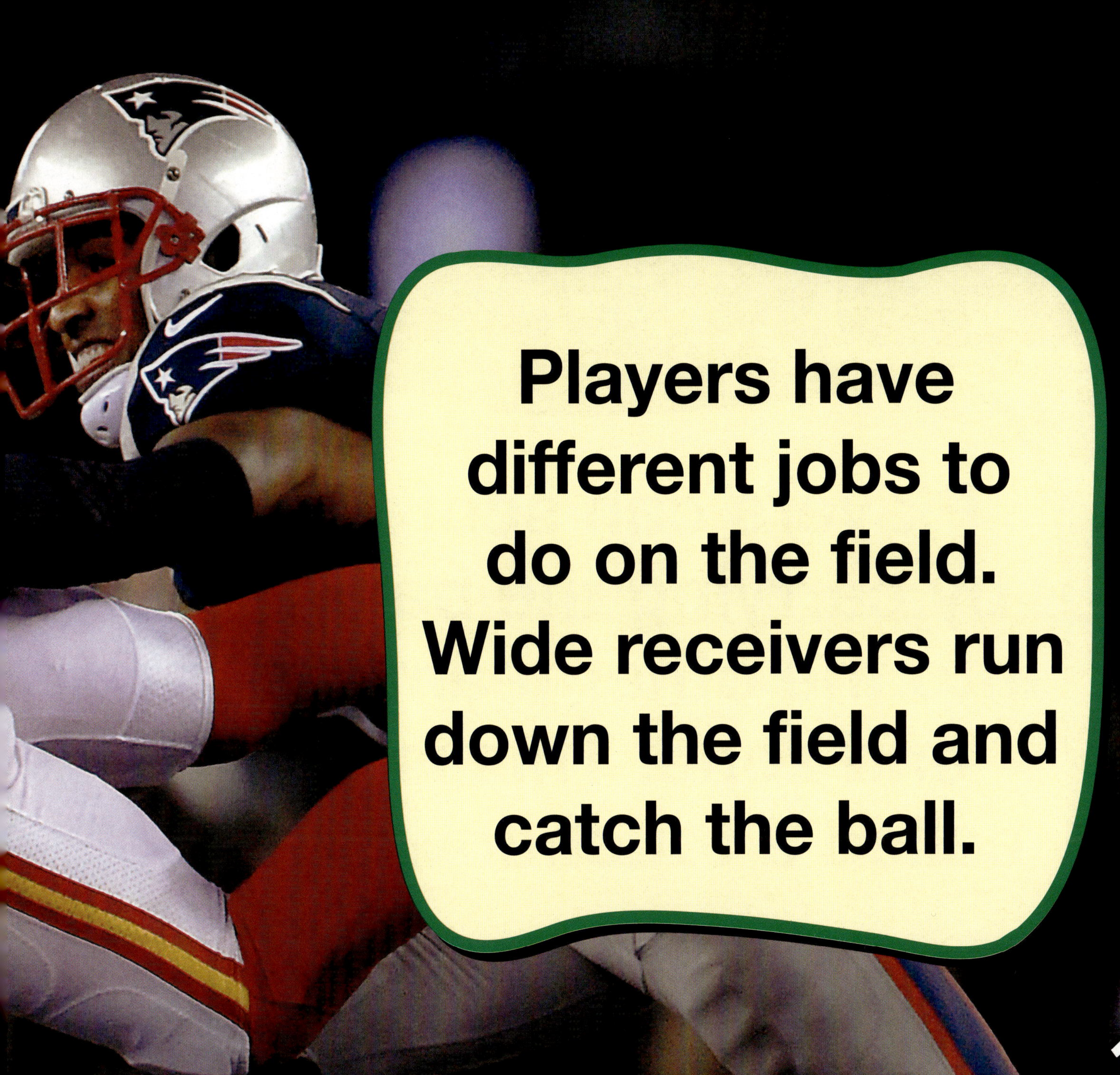

Players have different jobs to do on the field. Wide receivers run down the field and catch the ball.

Players can score by carrying the ball into the other team's end zone. This is called a touchdown.

10
G

They can also score by kicking the ball through the other team's goal post.

The best football players play in the National Football League. There are 32 NFL teams.

The most important trophy in the NFL is the Vince Lombardi Trophy. Winners of the Super Bowl get the trophy.

NFL

Football is a fun sport to watch and play. More than 100 million people watch the Super Bowl each year.

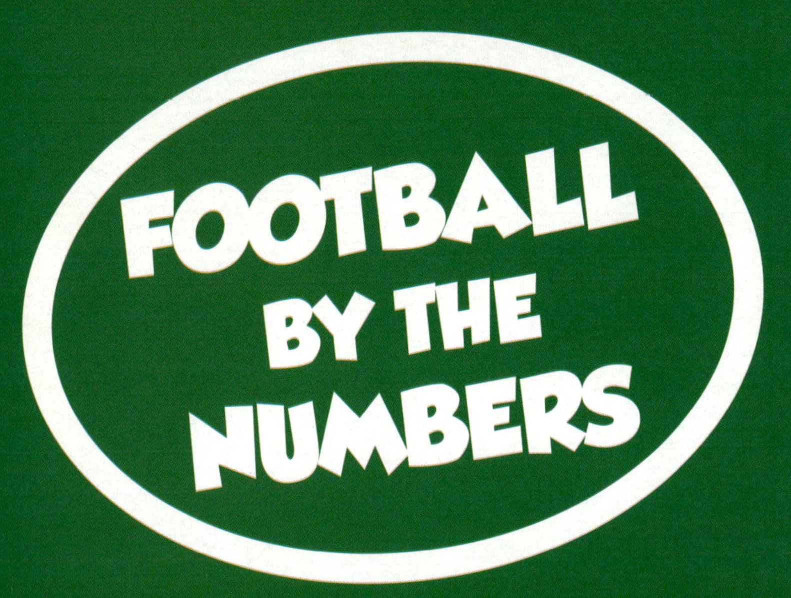

Each team can have **11** players on the **field** at once.

An **NFL** game is made up of **four 15-minute** quarters.

A **touchdown** is worth **6 points**. A **7th** point is earned by **kicking** a ball through the **goal posts**.

The first **Super Bowl** was played in **1967**.

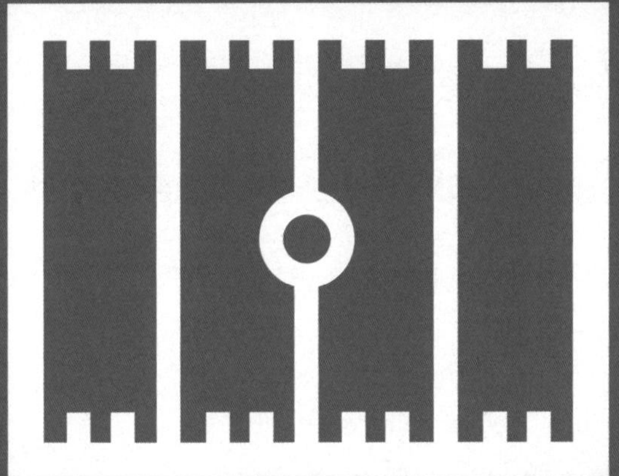

An **NFL field** is **120 yards** long, including end zones. (110 meters)

Each **NFL team** plays **16 games** in the regular season.

KEY WORDS

Research has shown that as much as 65 percent of all written material published in English is made up of 300 words. These 300 words cannot be taught using pictures or learned by sounding them out. They must be recognized by sight. This book contains 35 common sight words to help young readers improve their reading fluency and comprehension. This book also teaches young readers several important content words, such as proper nouns. These words are paired with pictures to aid in learning and improve understanding.

Page	Sight Words First Appearance
4	in, is, most, of, one, the
7	a, and, their, to
8	by
11	different, do, down, have, on, run
12	can, end, into, other, this
15	also, they, through
16	are, play, there
18	get, important
20	each, more, people, than, watch

Page	Content Words First Appearance
4	football, sports, United States
7	bodies, heads, helmets, pads, players
8	ball, carrying, catching, kicking, throwing
11	field, wide receivers
12	end zone, touchdown
15	goal, post
16	National Football League
18	Super Bowl, Vince Lombardi Trophy

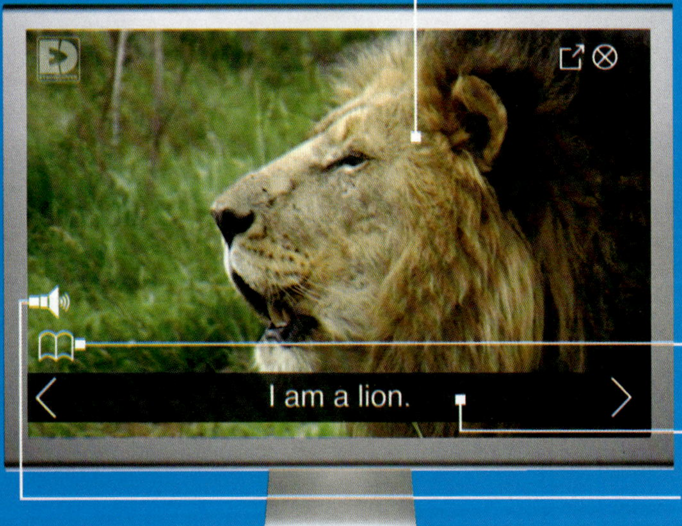

Watch
Video content brings each page to life.

Browse
Thumbnails make navigation simple.

Read
Follow along with text on the screen.

Listen
Hear each page read aloud.

Go to www.eyediscover.com and enter this book's unique code.

BOOK CODE

AVM75328